Isolation Boredom Busters

By Dr Zewlan Moor

Illustrated by Clarice Masajo

Library For All Ltd.

Isolation Boredom Busters

First published 2022

Published by Library For All Ltd
Email: info@libraryforall.org
URL: libraryforall.org

This book was made possible by the generous support of the June Canavan Foundation.

Original illustrations by Clarice Masajo

Isolation Boredom Busters
Dr Moor, Zewlan
ISBN: 978-1-922827-27-2
SKU04096

Isolation Boredom Busters

Sometimes we need to isolate. 'Isolate' means to stay inside, away from other people, and away from touching things other people will touch.

We need to do this if we are sick with a virus. This will stop the spread of the virus to other people.

It can be boring and lonely if you are isolated by yourself. But there are things you can do to help pass the time.

1

Plan your time: You might like
to draw up a calendar and mark
off the days. Or you can mark off
the days by making tally marks on
the ground.

2

Design your own games and
puzzles: Even a collection of
simple stones can be used to play
make-believe games, like schools,
battles or sports.

You can also make competitions
for yourself. Practise throwing a
pebble into a circle on the ground.
Gradually move further and further
away, until it is super-challenging.
Try it with all different sized
pebbles and from different angles.

3

Spread out your games and activities so you have something to look forward to every day.

4

Tell yourself stories: You can act out the various parts and do different voices. If you have pencils and paper, record these stories in words or pictures.

5

Keep your body healthy by exercising: Design a routine of sit-ups, push-ups, and running on the spot. These are all exercises you can do anywhere with no equipment. If you do enough of them and push yourself to go faster, you will keep your heart rate up and stay healthy.

If you can get out in the fresh air and sunshine to get some exercise, this is even better. Just stay 1.5 metres away from everyone else.

6

Help calm your mind: Relax by counting to six when you breathe in and out. This can also help you get a good night's sleep.

If you are isolated as a family it is a bit easier. Some communities call this a 'bubble' of people that you are allowed to talk to and play with.

You might like to start a project with your bubble people, like planting vegetables and herbs for your family.

Ask people, like family members, to help you learn how to do that.

Maybe other people in your bubble have special skills they can teach you.

This might be your one big chance in life to learn how to sew and knit, how to cook and clean, or how to wash your clothes.

You might notice that other people in your household are also sad and scared. They might even act out their feelings by being grumpy or angry. This is probably a result of being in isolation, not because of anything you have done.

Maybe, when they are feeling less stressed, you can invite them to join you in doing some of the activities that you enjoy.

You could challenge someone to a game of pebbles, and show them just how good you are now.

You could tell them a story or act out one of the plays you have invented.

25

Or you could teach them deep breathing exercises to help calm them down and feel more relaxed.

Who knows? Perhaps your time in isolation is the time for you to take on the role of Activities Coordinator in your house. Kids are the best people for that job—experts in play!

And remember, it might feel like your isolation will last forever, but it won't. One day soon the world will return to normal and you will be able to see your friends again.

You might even look forward to going back to school!

Do you think you will?

You can use these questions to talk about this book with your family, friends and teachers.

What did you learn from this book?

Describe this book in one word. Funny? Scary? Colourful? Interesting?

How did this book make you feel when you finished reading it?

What was your favourite part of this book?

download our reader app
getlibraryforall.org

About the author

Dr Zewlan (pronounced "Shoolen") Moor is an Australian medical doctor and author whose passion for social justice was formed on childhood visits to family in the Philippines. The stark inequalities she saw at the age of 8 made a lasting impression. She is thrilled to be published by a publisher who embraces the United Nations Sustainable Development Goals—Library For All. It fulfils two long-held dreams: to contribute to international public health through health promotion; and to bring the joy of reading and language to all children.

Did you enjoy this book?

We have hundreds more expertly curated original stories to choose from.

We work in partnership with authors, educators, cultural advisors, governments and NGOs to bring the joy of reading to children everywhere.

Did you know?

We create global impact in these fields by embracing the United Nations Sustainable Development Goals.

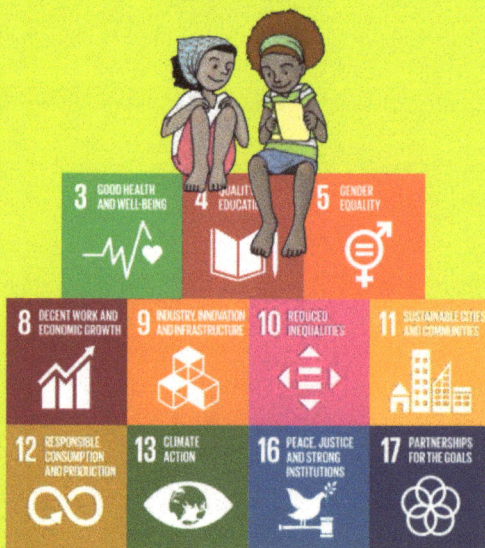

librariforall.org

www.ingramcontent.com/pod-product-compliance
Lightning Source LLC
Chambersburg PA
CBHW040313050426
42452CB00018B/2828